MIGHTY MACHINES

HELICOPTERS

by Wendy Strobel Dieker

AMICUS | AMICUS INK

rotor

cockpit

Look for these
words and pictures
as you read.

wheel

tail rotor

Look! Up in the sky!
It is a helicopter.

A helicopter can fly.

It can hover.

It can carry a truck! Wow!

See the rotor? It spins fast.
The helicopter goes straight up.

rotor

See the cockpit?
The pilot sits there.
She flies the helicopter.

cockpit

tail rotor

See the tail rotor?
It tilts.
It helps steer.

See the wheel?
It folds up in the air.
It comes down on land.

wheel

Oh no! A fire!

A helicopter drops water.

It helps put out the fire.

rotor

cockpit

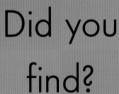

Did you find?

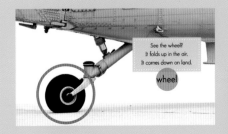

wheel

tail rotor

Spot is published by Amicus and Amicus Ink
P.O. Box 1329, Mankato, MN 56002
www.amicuspublishing.us

Library of Congress Cataloging-in-Publication Data
Names: Dieker, Wendy Strobel, author.
Title: Helicopters / by Wendy Strobel Dieker.
Description: Mankato, Minnesota : Amicus, [2020] | Series:
 Spot. Mighty machines | Audience: K to Grade 3.
Identifiers: LCCN 2018024491 (print) | LCCN
 2018036467 (ebook) | ISBN 9781681517278 (pdf)
 | ISBN 9781681516455 (library binding) | ISBN
9781681524313(pbk.)
Subjects: LCSH: Helicopters--Juvenile literature. |
 Helicopters--Parts--Juvenile literature. | CYAC: Helicopters.
 | LCGFT: Instructional and educational works. | Picture
 books. Classification: LCC TL716.2 (ebook) |
 LCC TL716.2 .D54 2020 (print) | DDC 629.133/352--dc23
LC record available at https://lccn.loc.gov/2018024491

Printed in China

HC 10 9 8 7 6 5 4 3 2 1
PB 10 9 8 7 6 5 4 3 2 1

Alissa Thielges, editor
Deb Miner, series designer
Aubrey Harper, book designer
Holly Young, photo researcher

Photos by Shutterstock/tai11 cover, 16;
iStock/breckeni 1; Getty/Lisa-Blue 3;
DOD/U.S. Air Force photo/Staff Sgt.
Patrick Harrower 4–5; iStock/Chris
Mansfield 6–7; Shutterstock/Benny
Marty 8–9; iStock/pichitstocker 10–11;
iStock/TommyIX 12–13; Shutterstock/
smikeymikey1 14–15

HELICOPTERS